BES Christ

New Gifts & Ideas

Your Promise of Success

Welcome to the world of Confident Cooking, created for you in
our test kitchen, where recipes are double tested by our team
of home economists to achieve a high standard of success.

MURDOCH BOOKS

Sydney • London • Vancouver

Christmas Menus

Cold Buffet for 12

Prawns with Fresh Herb Dip
Mushroom and Thyme Pâté
Glazed Leg of Ham
Chicken and Apricot Terrine
Vegetable Slaw with Mustard Mayonnaise
Leafy Green Salad with Walnut Dressing
Wild and Brown Rice Salad
Citrus Salad
Praline Chocolate Ice-cream Log
Tropical Fruit Pavlova Tower

Prawns with Fresh Herb Dip

Preparation time:
  30 minutes
Cooking time:
  5 minutes
Serves 12

1.5 kg cooked medium
  king prawns

Fresh Herb Dip
30 g butter
2 spring onions,
  chopped
2 garlic cloves, crushed
1 teaspoon sambal oelek
2 tablespoons chopped
  basil
2 tablespoons chopped
  parsley
2 tablespoons chopped
  mint
1 cup mayonnaise
½ cup thickened cream

1 Peel prawns leaving
tails intact, devein.
Store in refrigerator
until required.
2 **To make Dip:** Melt
butter in small pan, add
spring onions and
garlic, stir-fry over
medium heat until soft,
cool. Combine spring
onion mixture in a
medium bowl with
sambal oelek, basil,
parsley, mint,
mayonnaise and cream.
3 Serve Fresh Herb Dip
with prepared prawns.

♦ Unsuitable to freeze.

*Clockwise from top: Glazed Leg of Ham (p. 5),
Prawns with Fresh Herb Dip, Mushroom
and Thyme Pâté (p. 4)*

Mushroom and Thyme Pâté

Preparation time:
15 minutes
Cooking time:
12 minutes
Serves 12

60 g butter
1 small onion, chopped
1 garlic clove, crushed
1 tablespoon thyme
  leaves
250 g chicken livers,
  chopped
2 rashers bacon,
  chopped
60 g small mushroom
  caps
1/4 cup port
3/4 cup thickened cream

1 Melt butter in medium pan, add onion, garlic and thyme, stir-fry for 2 minutes or until onion is tender.
2 Add livers and bacon, stir-fry for 3 minutes or until browned. Add mushrooms and port, stir-fry 10 minutes or until most of the liquid has evaporated.
3 Place mixture into blender or food processor bowl, add cream, process to a smooth texture. Spoon into serving dish. Store, covered with plastic wrap, in refrigerator until needed.

Note: Pâté can be made up to 1 week ahead.
◆ Unsuitable to freeze.
◆ Serve with crackers or vegetable straws.

1. Glazed Leg of Ham. Remove rind gently with your hands.

2. Cut the rind of large orange into long, thin strips.

3. Add water, orange rind and cloves to baking dish.

4. Using a sharp knife, score the fat with deep cuts.

Glazed Leg of Ham

Preparation time:
 10 minutes
Cooking time:
 3 hours 45 minutes
Serves 20

1 x 7 kg leg ham
1 large orange
2 cups water
6 whole cloves
1¼ cups soft brown
 sugar, firmly packed
1 tablespoon mustard
 powder
1 cup orange
 marmalade or
 apricot jam
extra whole cloves

1 Preheat oven to moderate 180°C. Remove rind from ham by running a thumb around the edge, under the rind. Begin pulling from the widest edge. When rind has been removed to within 10 cm of the shank end, cut through the rind around the shank. Using a sharp knife, remove excess fat from ham; discard. Squeeze juice from orange and set aside.

2 Cut orange rind into long, thin strips.

3 Place ham on a roasting rack in deep baking dish; add water, peel and cloves to dish. Cover ham and dish securely with foil; cook for 2 hours.

4 Remove from oven. Drain meat and discard pan juices. Using a sharp knife, score the fat with deep cuts crossways and then diagonally to form a diamond pattern.

5 Combine the sugar, mustard and marmalade in a medium bowl; mix to a thick paste. Spread half thickly over the ham. Return to a moderately hot oven 210°C, and cook, uncovered, for about 30 minutes.

6 Combine orange juice with remaining brown sugar paste; stir until smooth. Remove ham from oven; brush with a little brown sugar mixture. Press a clove into each diamond, return to oven. Roast, uncovered, for a further hour; brush with the brown sugar mixture every 10 minutes. Serve ham sliced, warm or cold.

Note: Cover leftover ham with a damp cloth; store in refrigerator for about 10 days. Change cloth regularly.

5. *Combine the sugar, mustard and marmalade in a medium bowl.*

6. *Press a clove into each diamond, return ham to the oven.*

Chicken and Apricot Terrine

Preparation time: *1 hour*
Cooking time:
  1 hour 15 minutes
Serves 12

500 g dried apricots
1 cup (160 g) pinenuts
⅓ cup oil
2 large onions, chopped
2 cups (about 125 g)
  fresh white
  breadcrumbs
⅔ cup chopped parsley
2 eggs, lightly beaten
2 tablespoons oil, extra
60 g butter
12 chicken breast fillets
2 tablespoons gelatine
2 cups light chicken
  stock

1 Preheat oven to moderate 180°C. You will need 2 loaf tins measuring 21 x 14 x 7 cm. Place apricots in medium bowl, pour over boiling water, stand for 10 minutes, drain, then chop apricots roughly.
3 Place pinenuts in small dry pan, stir over medium heat until lightly golden, cool.
4 Heat oil in medium pan, add onion, stir-fry until soft, remove from heat, stir in apricots, pinenuts, breadcrumbs, parsley and egg.
5 Heat extra oil and butter in a large pan, add 4 chicken fillets. Cook over medium heat for about 4 minutes on each side or until almost cooked through. Remove from pan, drain on absorbent paper. Repeat with remaining chicken.
6 Using a sharp knife, carefully cut each fillet horizontally into 3 slices.
7 Divide apricot mixture and chicken into two equal portions. Arrange ¼ chicken slices from one portion, browned side down, over base of one loaf pan. Spread with ⅓ of apricot mixture from one portion. Repeat layering using chicken slices and apricot mixture from one portion, ending with chicken, browned side up. Repeat with remaining portion of chicken and apricot mixture to give two terrines.
8 Cover terrines with aluminium foil, place into a shallow baking dish. Pour in enough boiling water to come halfway up sides of terrines. Bake for 1 hour 15 minutes or until firm, cool. Cover with plastic wrap,

Chicken and Apricot Terrine (left), Vegetable Slaw with Mustard Mayonnaise (page 8)

refrigerate until cold.
9 Turn terrines out, wash loaf tins, return terrines to tins. Combine gelatine with stock in a small bowl. Stand bowl in hot water, stir until gelatine dissolves. Spoon evenly over terrines, cover with plastic wrap, refrigerate until set. Turn terrines out of loaf tins, slice and serve.

Note: Terrines can be made up to 2 days ahead.
◆ Unsuitable to freeze.

Vegetable Slaw with Mustard Mayonnaise

Preparation time:
20 minutes
Cooking time: *Nil*
Serves 12

3 cups finely sliced green cabbage
3 cups finely sliced red cabbage
2 red onions, finely sliced
3 large carrots, grated
3 large zucchini, grated

Mustard Dressing
1/2 cup mayonnaise
1/4 cup chopped parsley
3 garlic cloves, crushed
1 1/2 tablespoons seeded mustard

1 Layer green and red cabbage, onion, carrots and zucchini carefully in serving bowl.
2 To make Mustard Dressing: Combine mayonnaise, parsley, garlic and mustard in small bowl.
3 Spoon Mustard Dressing over salad, store covered with plastic wrap in refrigerator. Toss Slaw just before serving.

Note: Slaw can be made a day ahead.
◆ Unsuitable to freeze.

Leafy Green Salad with Walnut Dressing

Preparation time:
10 minutes
Cooking time: *Nil*
Serves 12

500 g English spinach
125 g rocket (arugola)
1 small cos lettuce
2 cups snow pea sprouts
1 1/2 cups flat-leafed parsley

Dressing
1/2 cup olive oil
1/3 cup walnut oil
1/3 cup white wine vinegar
2 garlic cloves, crushed
2 teaspoons French mustard

1 Combine spinach, rocket, cos, sprouts and parsley in a large bowl.
2 To make Dressing: Place oil, walnut oil, vinegar, garlic and mustard in a small jar. Shake for 20 seconds or until combined.
3 Add dressing to prepared salad, toss until combined.

Note: Rocket is a salad herb with a strong taste. You can grow it in temperate climates, or buy it from some large greengrocers. Snow pea sprouts are usually sold in plastic containers at greengrocers. If these vegetables are not available, replace with other green salad vegetables and herbs.
◆ Unsuitable to freeze.

Wild and Brown Rice Salad

Preparation time:
15 minutes
Cooking time:
35 minutes
Serves 12

3 cups wild and brown rice mix
1/4 cup sesame oil
12 spring onions, chopped
2 cobs corn, kernels removed
1 large capsicum, seeded and chopped
1/2 cup chopped parsley

Dressing
3/4 cup oil

Clockwise from left: Citrus Salad (p. 10), Leafy Green Salad with Walnut Dressing, Wild and Brown Rice Salad

2 tablespoons white
  wine vinegar
1 tablespoon curry
  powder
1 tablespoon sugar
1 tablespoon grated
  ginger

1 Add rice mix to large
pan of boiling water,
simmer over medium
heat for 30 minutes or
until tender, drain, rinse
under cold water.
2 Heat oil in medium
pan, add spring onion,
corn kernels and
capsicum, stir-fry over
medium heat 2 minutes
or until tender.
3 Combine rice,
vegetables and parsley
in large mixing bowl.
4 To make Dressing:
Place oil, vinegar, curry
powder, sugar and
ginger in a small jar.
Shake vigorously for 20
seconds or until
mixture is combined.
Add dressing to salad,
stir until all ingredients
are combined.

9

Note: This salad can be made completely a day ahead. Cover with plastic wrap, store in refrigerator. Stir well just before serving. Wild and brown rice mix is available from supermarkets.
◆ Unsuitable to freeze.

Citrus Salad

Preparation time:
  20 minutes
Cooking time: *Nil*
Serves 12

2 large oranges
2 large grapefruit
2 large tangelos
12 radishes, sliced
1 Spanish onion, thinly
  sliced
1 telegraph cucumber,
  sliced
1/2 cup coriander
  leaves

Dressing
1/2 cup olive oil
2 tablespoons rice wine
  vinegar
3 teaspoons soy sauce
1 teaspoon sambal oelek

1 Peel rind and pith from oranges, grapefruit and tangelos, cut fruit into 3 mm slices, remove seeds.
2 Combine fruit slices in a large bowl with radish, onion, cucumber and coriander.
3 To make Dressing: Place oil, vinegar, soy

sauce and sambal oelek in a small jar. Shake vigorously for 20 seconds or until combined. Pour over salad just before serving.

Note: Sambal oelek is a fiery mixture of crushed chillies and salt, available from supermarkets.
◆ Unsuitable to freeze.

Praline Chocolate Ice-cream Log

Preparation time: *1 hour*
Cooking time: *Nil*
Serves 12

Almond Praline
2/3 cup slivered
  almonds
2/3 cup sugar

Ice-cream mixture
1 cup dried mixed
  fruit
1/3 cup sweet sherry
4 litres vanilla
  ice-cream
2 x 200 g rolls almond
  paste
200 g dark chocolate,
  chopped
1 1/4 cups thickened
  cream, whipped

1 Line 2 loaf tins, 21 x 14 x 7 cm, smoothly with aluminium foil.
2 To make Almond

Praline: Scatter almonds on lightly oiled oven tray, bake in moderate oven 180°C for 10 minutes or until lightly browned, cool on tray. Place sugar in medium pan, heat gently without stirring until sugar begins to melt. Stir over low heat until evenly coloured and sugar has been dissolved (small-crack stage, 138°C on sugar thermometer). Remove from heat, pour evenly over almonds, allow to set, crush coarsely.
3 Combine mixed fruit and sherry in glass bowl, stand 2 hours. Soften one-third of the ice-cream, add crushed almond praline, reserving some larger pieces for decoration. Stir until combined. Divide mixture into loaf tins, freeze until firm.
4 Roll half of the almond paste into two rectangles large enough to cover ice-cream, return it to freezer.
5 Combine half remaining ice-cream and the chocolate in medium pan, stir over medium heat until chocolate has melted, pour into a bowl, freeze until semi-frozen. Divide between loaf tins, freeze until this

Praline Chocolate Ice-Cream Log (left), Tropical Fruit Pavlova Tower (p. 12)

layer is firm.

6 Roll remaining almond paste as above, place over chocolate layer, return to freezer.

7 Soften remaining ice-cream, add dried fruit mixture, stir until combined. Divide between loaf tins, freeze until firm.

8 To serve: Turn out onto serving plate, remove foil, pipe cream along the top of each log, sprinkle with the reserved almond praline.

Tropical Fruit Pavlova Tower

Preparation time:
45 minutes
Cooking time:
1 hour 30 minutes
Serves 12

8 egg whites
2½ cups caster sugar
250 g cream cheese, softened
1 tablespoon lemon juice

⅓ cup caster sugar, extra
1¼ cups thickened cream
1 small mango, puréed
500 g sliced mixed fresh fruit

1 Preheat oven to very slow 120°C. Brush three oven trays with melted butter or oil. Line each with paper, grease paper. Dust lightly with sifted cornflour, shake off excess. Using plates or cake tins as guides, mark a 24 cm round on one tray. Mark an

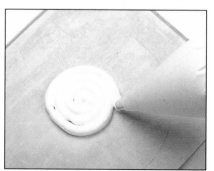

1. *Tropical Fruit Pavlova Tower. Mark rounds on floured tray with plate as guide.*

2. *Add sugar gradually to egg whites, beating constantly.*

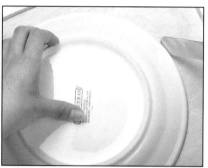

3. *Pipe meringue onto rounds to the sizes marked on trays.*

4. *Pipe about 20 small rounds with leftover meringue.*

18 cm, a 13 cm and a 7 cm round on another tray. Leave remaining tray unmarked.

2 Place egg whites in large, dry mixing bowl. Using electric beaters, beat egg whites until soft peaks form. Add sugar gradually, beating constantly until mixture is thick and glossy and all the sugar is dissolved.

3 Spoon mixture into a piping bag fitted with a large plain piping nozzle, pipe meringue into rounds on prepared trays.

4 Use leftover meringue to pipe about 20 rounds on remaining tray. Bake for 1 hour 30 minutes or until pale and crisp, alternating shelf positions occasionally during cooking. Remove from oven, cool on trays.

5 Using electric beaters, beat cream cheese, lemon juice and extra sugar in small mixing bowl until smooth. Beat cream in small bowl until soft peaks form, fold into cream cheese mixture with mango.

6 **To assemble tower:** Place large meringue layer on serving plate, spread with about 1 cup mango cream. Place 6 rounds around outside, about 3 cm in from the edge. Arrange some fruit around rosettes and in centre. top with 18 cm circle, spread with about 3/4 cup mango cream, 5 rounds and more fruit. Continue layering as above, reducing the quantity of cream, rosettes and fruit as you go. Top the smallest meringue layer with mango cream, fruit and one rosette.

Note: Meringue layers can be made up to one week ahead and stored in airtight container.
◆ Assemble up to 4 hours ahead, store in refrigerator.
◆ Mango cream can be made a day ahead.
◆ Use any fruit of your choice, e.g. mangoes, cherries, nectarines, apricots, berries. Canned or frozen fruit may also be used.

HINT
Care needs to be taken storing meringues in a humid climate. If you are making them the day before serving, leave the cooked meringues in the oven without opening the door until you're ready to assemble them. A meringue that has softened can be crisped successfully in a slow oven.

5. *Beat cream and fold into cream cheese mixture with mango.*

6. *Start assembling tower by spreading large meringue with mango cream.*

Hot Dinner for 6

Avocado Salad with Lemon Mustard Sauce
Lemony Roast Turkey
Fluffy Potatoes
Baby Squash with Bacon
Asparagus Bean Bundles
Golden Steamed Pudding
Lemon Mascarpone Custard

Avocado Salad with Lemon Mustard Sauce

Preparation time:
20 minutes
Cooking time: *Nil*
Serves 6

Lemon Mustard Sauce
*1 tablespoon lemon
juice*
*1 tablespoon tarragon
vinegar*
3 egg yolks
*1 teaspoon French
mustard*
125 g butter, melted

Salad
1 large carrot
3 spring onions
*2 avocados,
sliced*
1 mango, sliced
*6 canned artichoke
hearts, quartered*
½ cup watercress leaves

**1 To make Lemon
Mustard Sauce:**
Combine lemon juice,
vinegar, egg yolks and
mustard in a blender or
food processor bowl.
With motor constantly
operating, add hot,
bubbly butter in a thin
steady stream,
processing until all the
butter is added.
Transfer to small bowl,
cover with plastic wrap.
2 Cut carrot and spring
onions into very fine
strips, about 4 cm long.
3 Spoon sauce onto
serving plates, arrange
carrot and spring onion
in the centre. Top with
avocado, mango and
artichokes, garnish with
watercress.

*Clockwise from left: Avocado Salad with Lemon
Mustard Sauce, Lemony Roast Turkey (p. 16) on
platter with Asparagus Bean Bundles (p. 18), Baby
Squash and Bacon (p. 17), and Fluffy Potatoes (p. 17)*

1. *Lemony Roast Turkey. Mix together stuffing ingredients.*

2. *Pat turkey dry, inside and out, with absorbent paper.*

Lemony Roast Turkey

Preparation time:
20 minutes
Cooking time: *2 hours*
Serves 6

Lemon Stuffing
3 cups (about 180 g) fresh white breadcrumbs
500 g sausage mince
2 medium white onions, chopped
2 tablespoons chopped rosemary
2 garlic cloves, crushed
1/4 cup lemon juice
2 teaspoons grated lemon rind
1/2 cup slivered almonds

1 x 3 kg turkey
60 g butter, melted
1 lemon, sliced
2 1/2 cups light chicken stock
1 1/2 cups white wine
2 tablespoons plain flour

1/3 cup water
cranberry jelly for serving

1 Preheat oven to moderately slow 160°C.
To make stuffing: Combine breadcrumbs in medium bowl with sausage mince, onions, rosemary, garlic, lemon juice, lemon rind and almonds. Discard turkey neck, pat turkey dry with absorbent paper. Spoon Lemon Stuffing into turkey, tie wings and drumsticks securely in place. Place on roasting rack over shallow baking dish, brush turkey with half the butter, lay lemon slices over breast. Pour stock and wine into baking dish. Cover turkey and dish with aluminium foil.
2 Bake for 1 hour 15 minutes. Remove foil and lemon slices, brush with remaining butter. Return to oven

for 45 minutes. To test if turkey is cooked, pierce the thigh with a skewer. If juice runs clear, turkey is ready. If still pink, continue cooking for about 10 minutes. Remove from oven, leave, covered with foil, in a warm place for 10 minutes.
3 Strain pan juices, return to baking dish. Blend flour with water in small bowl or jug until smooth. Add to juices in pan, stir over medium heat for 2 minutes or until gravy boils and thickens, boil 2 minutes.
4 Remove string from turkey, carve, serve with stuffing, gravy and cranberry jelly.

Note: Stuffing can be made a day ahead.
◆ Unsuitable to freeze.
◆ Make sure frozen turkey is completely thawed before cooking.

3. *Brush turkey with butter, lay lemon slices over breast.*

4. *Add blended flour and water to juices in the pan.*

Baby Squash and Bacon

Preparation time:
  5 minutes
Cooking time:
  10 minutes
Serves 6

*200 g yellow baby
  squash
125 g cherry tomatoes
3 rashers bacon, finely
  chopped
60 g butter
1 leek, sliced
1/4 cup chives, cut into
  2.5 cm lengths*

1 Cut each squash in halves or, if larger, in quarters. Halve the cherry tomatoes.
2 Stir-fry bacon in small pan over medium heat for 2 minutes or until it is golden and crisp, drain on absorbent paper.
3 Heat butter in medium pan, add squash and leek, stir-fry over medium heat until tender. Add tomatoes, stir-fry until heated through but not mushy. Serve sprinkled with chopped bacon and chives.

Note: This recipe is best cooked just before serving.
◆ Unsuitable to freeze.

Fluffy Potatoes

Preparation time:
  15 minutes
Cooking time:
  20 minutes
Serves 6

*3 medium pontiac
  potatoes, chopped
3 medium carrots,
  chopped
1/4 cup sour cream
1/4 cup grated
  fresh Parmesan
  cheese
freshly ground black
  pepper*

*2 teaspoons sesame
  seeds
chilli powder*

1 Preheat oven to moderate 180°C. Brush an oven tray with melted butter or oil. Cook potatoes and carrots in simmering water until tender, drain, mash well with a masher or fork. Add sour cream, cheese and pepper.
2 Pile 1/4 cup of mixture onto prepared tray, use a fork to rough up the surface. Make three similar size mounds with the rest of the mixture.
3 Sprinkle each mound with sesame seeds and a pinch of chilli. Bake for 30 minutes or until lightly browned.

Note: This recipe can be prepared a day ahead, and baked just before serving.
◆ Unsuitable to freeze.

Asparagus Bean Bundles

Preparation time:
  10 minutes
Cooking time: *5 minutes*
Serves 6

300 g asparagus
300 g beans
6 long chives
90 g butter

1 Cut asparagus in half. Trim tops and tails of beans, trim to same length as asparagus.
2 Bring a medium pan of water to the boil, add asparagus, cook 2 minutes or until tender but not soft, lift out, rinse under cold water, drain. Repeat procedure with beans.
3 Gather asparagus and beans together in six equal bundles, wrap a chive around each bundle, tie carefully with a knot.
4 Melt butter in large pan, add bundles, cover, cook over medium heat for 3 minutes or until heated through, turn occasionally.

Note: Bundles can be prepared to end of Step 3 up to a day ahead. Store, covered with plastic wrap, in refrigerator, until time to cook.
◆ Unsuitable to freeze.

Golden Steamed Pudding

Preparation time:
  20 minutes
Cooking time: *4 hours*
Serves 6

185 g butter
³⁄4 cup caster sugar
3 eggs
¹⁄3 cup chopped glacé cherries
¹⁄3 cup chopped glacé apricots
¹⁄3 cup chopped glacé pineapple
¹⁄4 cup chopped dried dates
¹⁄4 cup sultanas
¹⁄4 cup mixed peel
¹⁄3 cup chopped walnuts
1 cup plain flour
¹⁄2 teaspoon bicarbonate of soda

1 Brush an 8-cup capacity pudding basin or steamer with melted butter or oil. Line base with paper, grease paper. Grease a large sheet of aluminium foil and a large sheet of greaseproof paper. Lay paper over foil, greased side up. Pleat both sheets in the centre.
2 Using electric beaters, beat butter and sugar in small mixing bowl until light and creamy. Add eggs gradually, beating thoroughly after each addition.
3 Transfer mixture to large mixing bowl, add fruits, walnuts and sifted dry ingredients, stir until combined.
4 Spoon mixture into prepared basin. Cover with the greased foil and paper, greased side down. Place lid over foil, bring clips up and secure with string. If you have no lid, lay a pleated tea-towel over foil, tie it securely with string under the lip of the basin. Knot the four ends of the tea-towel together to form as a handle to lower the basin into the pan.
5 Place the basin on a trivet on a large, deep pan. Carefully pour boiling water down the side of the pan to come halfway up the side of the basin. Bring to the boil, cover, cook for 4 hours. Do not let the pudding boil dry, replenish with boiling water as the pudding cooks. Remove covering, invert pudding onto a plate. Serve with Lemon Mascarpone Custard.

Note: If not serving immediately, allow pudding to cool, store in refrigerator for up to 6 weeks. Reheat pudding by cooking the same way for 1 hour.
◆ Pudding can be frozen for up to 3 months.

Golden Steamed Pudding (left), Lemon Mascarpone Custard

Lemon Mascarpone Custard

Preparation time:
 5 minutes
Cooking time: *5 minutes*
Serves 6

2 tablespoons custard
 powder
1/3 cup sugar

1/2 cup orange juice
1 cup water
1/3 cup mascarpone
1/3 cup lemon butter
2 tablespoons Cointreau

1 Combine custard
powder and sugar in
medium pan, add
orange juice and water,
stir until combined. Stir
constantly over medium
heat for 3 minutes or
until mixture boils and
thickens, boil for a

further 1 minute.
2 Add mascarpone,
lemon butter and
Cointreau, stir until
heated through.

Note: Mascarpone is an
Italian fresh cream
cheese. It is extremely
rich and can be used as
a substitute for cream.
Available from
delicatessens and large
supermarkets.
◆ Unsuitable to freeze.

Quick Menu for 8

Asparagus with Tangy Herb Sauce
Roast Turkey Breast with Parsley Crust
Scalloped Potatoes and Leek
Crunchy Apple Salad
Storebought Christmas Pudding with
Rum Cream
Pistachio Orange Triangles

Asparagus with Tangy Herb Sauce

Preparation time:
10 minutes
Cooking time:
4 minutes
Serves 8

*6 x 250 g bunches
asparagus*
1/2 cup chopped chives

Tangy Herb Sauce
*1 cup watercress leaves,
stalks removed*
1/2 cup mint leaves
1 1/4 cups sour cream
1/3 cup cream
*1 tablespoon lemon
juice*

1 Add asparagus to a
pan of boiling water,
cook over high heat for
4 minutes or until
tender but not mushy,
drain.
2 To make **Tangy
Herb Sauce:** Combine
watercress and mint
leaves in blender or
food processor bowl,
blend 1 minute or until
finely chopped. Add
sour cream, cream and
lemon juice, blend
1 minute or until
combined. Transfer
mixture to medium
pan, stir over medium
heat for 3 minutes or
until hot.
3 Divide asparagus
into eight portions and
serve each with a
spoonful of Tangy Herb
Sauce, sprinkled with
chives.

Note: Sauce can be
made a day ahead.
Store, covered in plastic
wrap, in refrigerator.
Heat just before serving.
♦ Unsuitable to freeze.

*Asparagus with Tangy Herb Sauce (at front), Roast
Turkey Breast with Parsley Crust (p. 22)*

Roast Turkey Breast with Parsley Crust

Preparation time:
10 minutes
Cooking time:
45 minutes
Serves 8

1 kg turkey breast
supreme
1 egg, lightly beaten

Parsley Crust
60 g butter
4 spring onions, finely
chopped
2 garlic cloves, crushed
2 cups (about 125 g)
fresh white
breadcrumbs
2 tablespoons finely
chopped parsley

cranberry jelly to serve

1 Preheat oven to moderate 180°C. Place turkey in deep baking dish, pat dry with absorbent paper. Brush with egg.
2 To make Parsley Crust: Melt butter in small pan over medium heat. Add spring onions and garlic, stir until softened. Add breadcrumbs and parsley, stir until combined, cool.
3 Press Parsley Crust firmly onto turkey. Bake for 45 minutes or until crust is golden brown. Serve turkey sliced, with cranberry jelly.

Note: Crust can be made a day ahead.
◆ Turkey breast supreme is available from chicken shops and supermarkets.
◆ Unsuitable to freeze.

Scalloped Potatoes and Leek

Preparation time:
10 minutes
Cooking time: *1 hour*
Serves 8

8 medium (about 2 kg)
new potatoes,
scrubbed and thinly
sliced
4 leeks, sliced
freshly ground black
pepper
2 teaspoons dried
mixed herbs
1 cup chicken stock
125 g butter

1 Preheat oven to moderate 180°C. Place potato and leek slices in alternate layers in a shallow ovenproof dish, sprinkle each layer with pepper and herbs.
2 Pour over stock, dot with butter, cover with aluminium foil. Bake for 30 minutes, remove foil, bake further 30 minutes or until potatoes are tender.
◆ Unsuitable to freeze.

Crunchy Apple Salad

Preparation time:
15 minutes
Cooking time: *Nil*
Serves 8

2 red apples
4 sticks of celery
1 large red capsicum
250 g snow peas,
topped and tailed
1/2 cup bottled French
dressing
1/2 cup roasted unsalted
peanuts

1 Cut apples into quarters, remove core, slice thinly. Cut celery sticks into straws 6 cm long. Halve capsicum, remove seeds, cut into 6 cm straws.
2 In a large mixing bowl combine apple, celery, capsicum and snow peas. Add dressing, toss well. Serve salad sprinkled with peanuts.

Note: Slice apples and add dressing just before serving.
◆ Unsuitable to freeze.

Scalloped Potatoes and Leek (left),
Crunchy Apple Salad

Storebought Christmas Pudding with Rum Cream

Preparation time:
5 minutes
Cooking time: *Nil for Rum Cream plus heating time for pudding*

1 Christmas pudding

Rum Cream
125 g cream cheese
60 g butter, softened
1/3 cup icing sugar
2 tablespoons dark rum
1 1/4 cups thickened cream

1 Reheat pudding following instructions on the packet.
2 To make Rum Cream: Using electric beaters, beat softened cream cheese, butter and icing sugar until light and creamy. Add rum and cream, beat for 1 minute or until soft peaks form.
3 Serve heated pudding with Rum Cream.

Note: Rum Cream can be made 2 days ahead. Bring it to room temperature before serving.
◆ Unsuitable to freeze.

Pistachio Orange Triangles

Preparation time:
15 minutes
Cooking time: *Nil*
Makes 56

1 cup Rice Bubbles
125 g plain, sweet biscuits, crushed
1/2 cup shredded coconut
1/2 cup chopped pistachio nuts
125 g butter, melted
1/2 cup condensed milk

Topping
125 g cream cheese, softened
1/4 cup icing sugar
2 teaspoons grated orange rind
2 tablespoons mixed peel, finely chopped
2 tablespoons pistachio nuts, extra, finely chopped

1 Brush a deep 29 x 19 x 3 cm Swiss roll tin with melted butter or oil. Line base and sides with aluminium foil, grease foil.
2 Combine Rice Bubbles, biscuit crumbs, coconut and pistachio nuts in a large mixing bowl. Add butter and condensed milk, stir until combined.
3 Press mixture evenly into prepared tin, smooth surface, refrigerate until firm.
4 To make Topping: Combine cream cheese, icing sugar and rind in a small bowl, stir until smooth. Spread over biscuit base using a flat-bladed knife, sprinkle evenly with peel and nuts, cover with plastic wrap, refrigerate until firm. Lift out of tin, cut into triangles. Store in airtight container.

Note: This slice can be stored in refrigerator.
◆ Unsuitable to freeze.

HINT
You may like to skin the pistachio nuts. To do this, cover the shelled nuts with boiling water and let them stand two or three minutes. Drain and let cool slightly, then simply rub the skin off with your fingers while the nuts are still warm.

Storebought Christmas Pudding with Rum Cream (at front), Pistachio Orange Triangles

Festive Lunch for 8

Capsicum, Eggplant and Pesto Terrine
Roast Duck with Mandarin Sauce
Roasted Tomatoes with Herbs
Snap Pea and Broad Bean Salad
Festive Fruity Potatoes
Raspberry Mousse Cake

Capsicum, Eggplant and Pesto Terrine

Preparation time:
30 minutes
Cooking time:
30 minutes
Serves 8

3 large red capsicums
750 g (about 2 small)
  eggplant
salt
1/3 cup oil
500 g English spinach
1/3 cup pesto

1 Preheat oven to moderate 180°C. Cut capsicums in half, remove seeds. Place them cut side down on an oven tray. Bake capsicum for 30 minutes or until skin blisters and browns. Cool and peel.
2 Cut eggplant into 5 mm slices, sprinkle with salt, stand 45 minutes. Rinse slices under cold water, drain, dry very well with absorbent paper.
3 Heat 1 tablespoon of the oil in pan, add a layer of eggplant slices. Cook over medium heat for 2 minutes on each side until lightly browned. Drain on absorbent paper. Repeat with remaining oil and eggplant.
4 Remove stalks from spinach leaves, place leaves in medium bowl, cover with hot water, stand 1 minute, drain, rinse under cold water. Line a 31 x 12 cm saddle tin with a double layer of spinach leaves, allowing leaves to drape over sides of tin.
5 Place a quarter of the eggplant in overlapping slices along the base of tin. Top with a third of the capsicum, spread with a quarter of the pesto. Repeat layering

Clockwise from left: Capsicum, Eggplant and Pesto Terrine, Roast Duck with Mandarin Sauce (p. 28), Roasted Tomatoes with Herbs (p. 29)

with remaining eggplant, capsicum and pesto.

6 Enclose filling completely with spinach leaves. Bake for 30 minutes or until tender, set aside to cool. Store terrine, covered with plastic wrap, in refrigerator. Turn out, serve sliced.

Note: Terrine can be made up to 2 days ahead.
◆ Unsuitable to freeze.
◆ Saddle tins (bar tins

with rounded, ridged base) are available from specialty kitchenware stores. If unavailable, use a loaf tin.
◆ Pesto is available in jars from supermarkets, delicatessens and pasta shops, or you can make your own.

Roast Duck with Mandarin Sauce

Preparation time:
30 minutes
Cooking time:
1 hour 40 minutes
Serves 8

3 x 1.6 kg ducks
60 g butter, melted

Stuffing
90 g butter
12 spring onions,
chopped

1. Roast Duck with Mandarin Sauce. Stir-fry vegetables, add breadcrumbs.

2. Spoon Stuffing into ducks, dividing it equally between each.

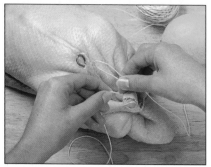

3. Tie wings and drumsticks of each duck securely in place.

4. For Sauce, blend cornflour and stock, add remaining ingredients.

3 garlic cloves, crushed
3 teaspoons grated
 ginger
8 cups (about 500 g)
 fresh white
 breadcrumbs
1/4 cup fresh chopped
 coriander
2 eggs, lightly beaten

Mandarin Sauce
1 x 310 g can mandarin
 segments
2 tablespoons cornflour
4 cups light chicken
 stock
1/2 cup orange juice
2 tablespoons lemon
 juice
1 tablespoon honey
1 tablespoon soy sauce
2 teaspoons grated
 ginger
1 tablespoon sugar

1 Preheat oven to
moderate 180°C. Rinse
ducks, pat dry with
absorbent paper.
2 **To make Stuffing:**
Heat butter in medium
pan, add spring onions,
garlic and ginger,
stir-fry for 3 minutes or
until soft, add
breadcrumbs, coriander
and eggs, stir until
combined. Remove
from heat.
3 Spoon Stuffing into
ducks, ensuring each
has the same amount.
4 Tie wings and
drumsticks securely in
place. Place ducks on
roasting rack over a
shallow baking dish,
brush with butter.
Roast for 1 hour, baste
ducks occasionally with
pan juices.
5 While ducks are
roasting, prepare
Mandarin Sauce.
Process undrained
mandarins to a smooth
texture in blender or
food processor. Place
cornflour in small pan,
add a little stock, stir
until smooth. Add
remaining stock, orange
and lemon juice, honey,
soy sauce, ginger, sugar
and mandarin purée,
stir over medium heat

until sauce boils and
thickens.
6 Remove ducks from
oven, drain pan juices,
place ducks in baking
dish, pour over
Mandarin Sauce. Roast
further 40 minutes. To
test if duck is cooked,
insert skewer into the
thigh. If juice runs clear,
duck is ready. Strain
sauce, serve with ducks.
◆ Unsuitable to freeze.

Roasted Tomatoes with Herbs

Preparation time:
 15 minutes
Cooking time:
 20 minutes
Serves 8

4 medium ripe tomatoes
2 teaspoons thyme
 leaves
sugar
salt
freshly ground black
 pepper

5. *Pour Mandarin Sauce over ducks,
roast further 40 minutes.*

6. *Insert a skewer in thigh; if juices run
clear, duck is cooked.*

Dressing
2 tablespoons olive oil
4 spring onions, finely
  chopped
2 garlic cloves, crushed
1 tablespoon balsamic
  vinegar
2 tablespoons shredded
  basil leaves

1 Preheat oven to moderate 180°C. Brush an oven tray with melted butter or oil. Place tomatoes in medium bowl, cover with boiling water, stand 1 minute, drain, rinse under cold water. Peel tomatoes, cut horizontally in half, scoop out seeds.
2 Place tomatoes, cut side up, on prepared tray, sprinkle with thyme, sugar, salt and pepper. Bake for 20 minutes or until tomatoes are tender but not mushy, cool.
3 To make Dressing: Heat oil in small pan, add spring onions and garlic, stir-fry over medium heat until soft, cool, stir in vinegar.
4 Serve tomatoes cut side down, spoon over dressing, sprinkle with shredded basil.

Note: Serve tomatoes at room temperature; they can be cooked up to 4 hours ahead. Spoon dressing over just before serving.
◆ Unsuitable to freeze.

Snap Pea and Broad Bean Salad

Preparation time:
  15 minutes
Cooking time: *Nil*
Serves 8

500 g shelled broad
  beans
250 g snap (sugar) peas
1/2 cup olive oil
4 leeks, sliced
4 garlic cloves, crushed
1 tablespoon French
  mustard
1 tablespoon balsamic
  vinegar
2 teaspoons sambal
  oelek or 1 small red
  chilli, finely chopped

1 Bring a pan of water to boil, add broad beans and snap peas, simmer for 2 minutes or until just tender, drain, rinse under cold water.
2 Heat oil in small pan, add leeks and garlic, stir-fry over high heat 2 minutes or until soft. Remove from heat, cool. Stir in mustard, vinegar and sambal oelek, add to broad beans and peas, stir until combined.

Note: Salad can be prepared up to 4 hours ahead. Stir well just before serving.

Festive Fruity Potatoes

Preparation time:
  20 minutes
Cooking time:
  45 minutes
Serves 8

4 medium new potatoes
  (about 1 kg)
1 kg kumera (orange
  sweet potato)
3/4 cup dried apricots
3/4 cup raisins
2/3 cup orange juice
60 g butter
2 tablespoons chopped
  chives

1 Preheat oven to moderate 180°C. Cut potato and kumera into 3 cm cubes. Cook in simmering water for 5 minutes, drain.
2 Combine apricots, raisins and orange juice in small pan, cover, bring to boil, remove from heat, stand 5 minutes.
3 Combine potatoes and undrained fruit in a shallow ovenproof dish, dot with butter. Bake for 45 minutes or until lightly browned. Stir occasionally. Garnish with chives.

Note: This dish can be prepared up to baking stage 4 hours ahead.

Snap Pea and Broad Bean Salad (top),
Fruity Potatoes

Raspberry Mousse Cake

Preparation time:
 45 minutes
Cooking time:
 15 minutes
Serves 8

Cake
*2 tablespoons plain
 flour
2 tablespoons
 self-raising flour
2 tablespoons cornflour
2 eggs
1/3 cup caster sugar*

Raspberry Mousse
*2 x 200 g punnets
 fresh or frozen
 raspberries
1 egg, extra
1/3 cup caster sugar,
 extra
250g packet cream
 cheese, softened
11/4 cups thickened
 cream
1 tablespoon gelatine
2 tablespoons water*

To Serve
icing sugar

1 Preheat oven to moderate 180°C. Brush a 20 cm round springform tin with melted butter or oil.
To make Cake: Sift flours and cornflour 3 times onto greaseproof paper.
2 Using electric beaters, beat eggs in small mixing bowl for 3 minutes or until thick and pale.
3 Add sugar gradually, beating constantly until dissolved and mixture is pale yellow and glossy. Transfer mixture to large mixing bowl.
4 Using a metal spoon, fold in dry ingredients quickly and lightly.
5 Spread mixture evenly into prepared tin. Bake for 15 minutes or until sponge is lightly golden and shrinks from side of tin. Leave sponge in the tin for 3 minutes before turning onto wire rack to cool.
6 **To make Raspberry Mousse:** Process 1 1/2 punnets raspberries to a smooth texture in blender or food processor bowl, pass through a fine sieve. Reserve half of the purée for serving.
7 Using electric beaters, beat extra egg and extra sugar in small bowl until creamy. Add cream cheese, beat until smooth. In a separate bowl beat cream until soft peaks form.
8 Combine gelatine with water in small bowl, stand bowl in hot water, stir until gelatine dissolves.
9 Using a metal spoon fold gelatine, half raspberry purée and reserved whole raspberries into cream cheese mixture, then fold in cream. Cover with plastic wrap, and refrigerate for

1. Raspberry Mousse Cake. Beat sugar into eggs until pale and glossy.

2. Spread cake mixture evenly into prepared tin.

Raspberry Mousse Cake

10 minutes or until mixture has thickened, stirring occasionally.
10 To assemble: Cut cake in half horizontally. Place first cake layer on a board. Spread cake evenly with mousse. Top with remaining cake layer, refrigerate until the mousse has set.
11 To serve: Sift icing sugar over top of cake, cut into wedges. Place onto serving plates and spoon reserved purée around cake.

Note: Raspberry Mousse Cake can be made a day ahead. Store, covered in plastic wrap, in refrigerator.
◆ Unsuitable to freeze.
◆ Serve with extra whole raspberries and ice-cream, if desired.

3. Add cream cheese to mousse mixture, beat until smooth.

4. Fold gelatine, half purée and whole raspberries into cream cheese mixture.

Gifts and Cakes

Some of the most welcome Christmas gifts are homemade and edible. The biscuits, chocolates, sweets and cakes in this chapter make delightful presents. Put them in a jar, tin or box, wrap them in pretty paper and remember to enclose heating or storage instructions if applicable.

Apple Fruitmince Tarts

Preparation time:
 30 minutes
Cooking time:
 15 minutes
Makes about 24

1½ cups plain flour
½ cup self-raising flour
125 g butter, chopped
2 teaspoons grated
 lemon rind
¼ cup water

Filling
1 small green apple,
 cored, peeled
410 g jar fruitmince
sugar for sprinkling

1 Preheat oven to moderately hot 210°C. Brush shallow patty tins with melted butter or oil. Sift plain and self-raising flours into mixing bowl, add chopped butter and lemon rind. Using fingertips, rub butter into flour until mixture is a fine, crumbly texture. Add almost all the water, mix to soft dough, adding more water if necessary. Turn onto lightly floured surface, knead 1 minute or until smooth. Remove one-third pastry, cover with plastic wrap, place in freezer. Cover remaining pastry with plastic wrap, refrigerate for 10 minutes.
2 Roll large portion of pastry out thinly. Cut into circles using a fluted 7 cm round cutter, press circles into prepared tins. Gather pastry scraps together, roll out and cut into

Clockwise from left: Apple Fruitmince Tarts, Liqueur Cream Sauce (p. 37), Panettone (p. 37), Apricot Chocolate Truffles (p. 36)

circles, as before. Add any leftover scraps to pastry in freezer.

3 To make filling: Grate apple coarsely, drain on absorbent paper. Combine apple and fruitmince. Place tablespoons of mixture into pastry cases. Coarsely grate frozen pastry, sprinkle over tarts. Sprinkle with sugar.

4 Bake for 15 minutes or until lightly browned, cool on racks.

Note: Store tarts in an airtight container for up to 2 weeks.

◆ Tarts can be frozen for up to 3 months.

HINT
Grated frozen pastry sprinkled with sugar makes a crisp topping for any sweet pie.

Apricot Chocolate Truffles

Preparation time: *30 minutes*
Cooking time: *Nil*
Makes about 25

1 cup Rice Bubbles
1/2 cup desiccated coconut
1/4 cup chopped dried apricots
1/4 cup chopped mixed peel
1/4 cup slivered almonds
3/4 cup sweetened condensed milk
250 g white chocolate, chopped
100 g dark chocolate, chopped
2 teaspoons white vegetable shortening

1 In a medium mixing bowl, combine Rice Bubbles, coconut, apricots, peel and almonds. Add condensed milk, stir until combined, cover with plastic wrap, refrigerate for until firm.

2 Shape heaped teaspoons of mixture into balls.

3 Place white chocolate in small heatproof bowl. Stand over pan of simmering water, stir until chocolate has melted and is smooth. Place a wire rack over an oven tray. Using two forks, dip truffles into chocolate, allow excess to run off, place onto wire rack, refrigerate until set.

4 Melt dark chocolate and white vegetable shortening as for Step 3, spoon over tops of truffles, allowing it to drizzle down sides. Refrigerate until set.

Note: Truffles can be decorated with chopped glacé cherries, toasted slivered almonds or miniature holly leaves.

◆ Unsuitable to freeze.

1. Apricot Chocolate Truffles. Mix together ingredients for centre of truffles.

2. Shape heaped teaspoons of mixture into balls.

Liqueur Cream Sauce

Preparation time:
10 minutes
Cooking time: *5 minutes*
Makes 3 cups

90 g butter
1 cup caster sugar
6 egg yolks
1/2 cup sweet sherry
1/2 cup brandy
1 1/4 cups thickened
  cream

1 Using electric beaters, beat butter and sugar in medium heatproof bowl. Add egg yolks, sherry, brandy and cream, beat until well combined.
2 Place bowl over pan of simmering water, stir 5 minutes or until mixture thickens slightly and coats the back of a wooden spoon with a creamy layer. Do not boil.

Note: Liqueur Cream Sauce can be stored in the refrigerator for up to 1 week.
◆ Unsuitable to freeze.

Panettone

Preparation time:
1 hour 30 minutes
Cooking time:
1 hour 15 minutes
Makes one 20 cm loaf

3/4 cup mixed fruit
2 tablespoons mixed peel
2 tablespoons orange
  juice
45 g fresh yeast
1 teaspoon sugar
2 tablespoons
  lukewarm water
3 cups plain flour
60 g butter
3 eggs, lightly beaten
2 tablespoons caster
  sugar
1/2 cup lukewarm milk
extra milk for glazing

1 Preheat oven to moderately hot 210°C.

Brush a 20 cm charlotte tin with melted butter or oil. Combine mixed fruit, peel and orange juice in a small bowl, stand while preparing rest of cake.
2 Combine yeast, sugar and water in a medium mixing bowl, blend until smooth. Stand, covered with plastic wrap, in warm place for about 10 minutes or until foamy.
3 Sift flour into large mixing bowl, add butter. Using fingertips, rub butter into flour for 2 minutes or until mixture is a fine, crumbly texture. Add fruit mixture, stir until well mixed.
4 Combine eggs, caster sugar and milk, stir in yeast mixture. Make a well in centre of flour, add yeast mixture. Using a knife, mix to a soft, wet dough.
5 Using your hand, vigorously beat dough

3. Using two forks, dip truffles into white chocolate.

4. Spoon melted dark chocolate over tops of truffles, letting it drizzle down sides.

for 5 minutes or until dough becomes slightly stringy, smooth and glossy. Scrape mixture down side of bowl. Leave, covered with plastic wrap, in warm place for 30 minutes or until well risen.

6 Repeat beating procedure for further 5 minutes, turn dough onto lightly floured surface, knead for 10 minutes or until dough is no longer sticky. Place into prepared tin, stand, covered with plastic wrap, in warm place for about 30 minutes or until well risen.

7 Brush with extra milk, bake for 15 minutes, reduce heat to moderate, 180°C, bake further 1 hour or until well browned and cooked through. When cooked, panettone will sound hollow when tapped. Turn onto wire rack to cool.

Note: If you don't have a charlotte tin, use an 8-cup pudding basin or a 20 cm round cake tin.
◆ Panettone is best eaten on day of baking, but it will stay fresh for up to 4 days, covered in plastic wrap.
◆ Can be frozen for up to 2 months.

Cherry Chocolates

Preparation time:
30 minutes
Cooking time: *Nil*
Makes about 40

125 g unsalted butter
2 cups icing sugar
1/3 cup thickened cream
2 cups desiccated coconut
pink food colouring
200 g glacé cherries
100 g dark chocolate, chopped
30 g white vegetable shortening
60 g white cooking chocolate

1 Heat butter in small pan until lightly browned, remove from heat. Add sifted icing sugar, cream, coconut and a few drops of food colouring, stir until combined.

2 Take about 2 teaspoons of mixture and press evenly around each cherry.

3 Place dark chocolate and shortening in small heatproof bowl. Stand over pan of simmering water, stir until the chocolate and shortening have melted and mixture is smooth.

4 Place a wire rack over an oven tray. Using two forks, dip cherries into chocolate, allow excess to run off, place cherries onto wire rack, allow to set.

5 Place white chocolate in small heatproof bowl. Stand over pan of simmering water, stir until chocolate has melted. Cool slightly and spoon into a small paper icing bag, seal open end. Snip tip off bag, drizzle white chocolate decoratively over cherry chocolates, allow to set.

Note: Cherry Chocolates can be stored in an airtight container in refrigerator for up to 2 weeks.

HINTS

An easy piping bag can be made by spooning mixture into the corner of a small plastic bag. Twist the open end to seal it and snip off corner of bag.
◆ ◆ ◆
Chocolate may also be melted in the microwave. It takes only a very few seconds, however – too long and it will burn. Microwave-melted chocolate doesn't look melted until you stir it.

Clockwise from left: Cherry Chocolates, Gingerbread Christmas Tree (p. 40), Apricot & Lemon Jam (p. 41)

Gingerbread Christmas Tree

Preparation time: *1 hour*
Cooking time:
  15 minutes
Makes 1 tree about
  25 cm high

125 g butter
1/2 cup caster sugar
1 egg yolk
1/4 cup honey
2 cups plain flour
1 teaspoon bicarbonate
  of soda

2 teaspoons ground
  ginger
mixed colour cachous
1 egg white
1 1/2 cups pure icing
  sugar, approximately
5 honey ice-cream cones
pure icing sugar for
  dusting

1 Preheat oven to moderate 180°C. Brush oven trays with melted butter or oil. Using electric beaters, beat butter and sugar in small mixing bowl until light and creamy. Add egg yolk and syrup, beat until combined.
2 Add sifted flour, soda and ginger, press together to form a soft dough. Turn onto lightly floured surface, knead 1 minute until smooth. Leave, covered with plastic wrap, in refrigerator 15 minutes.
3 Roll dough out to about 3 mm thick, between two sheets of baking paper. Cut 30 Christmas tree shapes from the dough using an 8 cm cutter. Re-roll

1. Gingerbread Christmas Tree. Add egg yolk and honey to creamed mixture.

2. Cut six star shapes from the remaining dough, using a 4 cm cutter.

3. Press a cachou onto the top of each tree and onto one point of each star.

4. Add sifted icing sugar to egg white, 1 tablespoon at a time.

the dough scraps and re-use. Cut six star shapes from the remaining dough, using a 4 cm cutter. Place on prepared trays, allowing room to spread. Press cachous onto the top of each tree and onto one point of each star. Bake for 15 minutes or until lightly golden, cool on wire rack.

4 Using electric beaters, beat egg white until slightly frothy. Add sifted icing sugar, 1 tablespoon at a time, beating until smooth between additions. Add enough icing sugar to give a stiff spreading consistency.

5 To assemble tree: Stack cones on top of each other spreading a little icing between each to join them together. Starting with the bottom cone, spread icing thickly. Press Christmas tree and star

biscuits into the icing, stacking biscuits in overlapping layers around the cone. Work your way up the cones in this manner, spreading with icing as you go. Leave room at the top, spread with icing. Press two stars, standing upright back to back, on the top. Sift extra icing sugar over tree.

Note: If biscuits won't adhere to cones, add more sifted icing sugar to icing to give a stiffer consistency.

♦ Biscuits can be made up to 2 days ahead, store in an airtight container. Once assembled, cover tree with plastic wrap until serving time.

♦ Unsuitable to freeze.

Apricot and Lemon Jam

Preparation time:
15 minutes
Cooking time: *1 hour*
Makes about 3 cups

500 g dried apricots
9 cups water
5 lemons
8 cups sugar

1 Soak apricots in half the water overnight. Boil whole lemons, uncovered, in remaining water until soft. Remove lemons and retain water. When cold, slice lemons thinly, removing pips and setting aside.

2 Boil apricots in their soaking water until tender, add sugar and sliced lemons, together with the reserved water and pips. (Tie the pips in a small muslin square.) Boil until the

5. Stack cones on top of each other, spreading a little icing between.

6. Press Christmas tree biscuits into the icing.

jam thickens and a teaspoon of the mixture placed on a sauce wrinkles when it is pushed with your finger.
3 Remove pips and spoon jam into sterilised jars. Seal while still hot.

Crispy Milk Truffles

Preparation time:
10 minutes
Cooking time: *Nil*
Makes about 24

250 g milk chocolate, roughly chopped
few drops peppermint essence
1½ cups fried unflavoured egg noodles

1 Cover an oven tray with a sheet of baking paper. Place chocolate in a medium heatproof bowl. Stand over pan of simmering water, stir until chocolate has melted and mixture is smooth, remove it from heat.
2 Add peppermint essence and noodles, stir until combined.
3 Place heaped teaspoons of mixture onto prepared tray, refrigerate until set.

Note: Noodles are available from

supermarkets and Asian food stores.

Note: Either dark or white chocolate can be used instead of milk chocolate, if preferred.
◆ Unsuitable to freeze.
◆ Truffles can be stored in an airtight container in refrigerator for up to 2 weeks

Rocky Road

Preparation time:
30 minutes
Cooking time:
20 minutes
Makes one 25 cm round

2 tablespoons gelatine
1½ cups water
2 cups sugar
pink food colouring
½ cup unsalted roasted peanuts
⅓ cup chopped glacé cherries
¾ cup desiccated coconut
500 g milk chocolate, roughly chopped

1 Cover an oven tray with a sheet of baking paper. Sprinkle gelatine over ½ cup of the water, stir until combined. Combine remaining water and sugar in a medium pan, stir over medium heat without boiling until sugar has completely dissolved. Bring to the boil, reduce heat to low,

add gelatine mixture, stir until combined, cook uncovered for 10 minutes, cool mixture to lukewarm.
2 Pour mixture into a large mixing bowl. Using electric beaters, beat on high speed for 8 minutes or until mixture is white and very thick.
3 Pour half of the mixture into a loaf tin. Add a few drops of food colouring to remaining mixture, stir until combined, pour into another loaf tin. Refrigerate both mixtures until set. Turn out, cut into 3 cm cubes.
4 In a large mixing bowl, combine the cubes of marshmallow, the peanuts, cherries and coconut.
5 Place chocolate in a medium heatproof bowl. Stand over pan of simmering water, stir until chocolate has melted and the mixture is smooth. Add to marshmallow mixture. Stir until well combined, spoon onto prepared tray, refrigerate until set.

Note: For ease of melting and mixing, use milk cooking chocolate.
◆ Can be stored, covered in plastic wrap, in refrigerator for up to 2 weeks.
◆ Unsuitable to freeze.

Clockwise from left: Crispy Milk Truffles, Mandarin and Passionfruit Butter, Rocky Road

Mandarin and Passionfruit Butter

Preparation time:
 5 minutes
Cooking time: 6 minutes
Makes 2 cups

4 eggs, lightly beaten
2/3 cup sugar
1/3 cup passionfruit pulp
3 tablespoons mandarin
 juice
125 g unsalted butter,
 roughly chopped

1 Combine eggs, sugar, passionfruit pulp, mandarin juice and butter in a medium heatproof bowl.
2 Place bowl over pan of simmering water, stir constantly for about 6 minutes or until mixture thickens slightly and thinly coats the back of a wooden spoon. Pour into hot, sterilised jars, seal while hot.

Note: Do not allow mixture to boil as curdling will result.
◆ Store in refrigerator for up to 3 weeks.

43

Chocolate Super Cookies

Preparation time:
15 minutes
Cooking time:
10 minutes
Makes about 30

125 g butter
100 g dark chocolate,
  roughly chopped
1 cup brown sugar
2 eggs, lightly beaten
1 cup plain flour
½ cup cocoa powder
½ cup roughly chopped
  unsalted, roasted
  macadamia nuts
⅓ cup sultanas
100 g white chocolate,
  roughly chopped
100 g milk chocolate,
  roughly chopped

1 Preheat oven to moderately hot 210°C. Brush oven trays with melted butter or oil. Melt butter in small pan, add dark chocolate, stir over low heat until melted. Transfer to large bowl.
2 Add sugar and eggs, stir until combined. Add sifted flour and cocoa, nuts, sultanas, white and milk chocolate, stir until combined.
3 Drop tablespoons of mixture onto prepared tray, allowing room for spreading. Bake for 10 minutes or until just set. Transfer cookies to wire rack to cool.

Note: Store cookies in an airtight container for up to 1 week.
◆ Can be frozen for up to 2 months.

Chilli Cheese Biscuits

Preparation time:
15 minutes
Cooking time:
15 minutes
Makes about 25

1 cup plain flour
¼ cup self-raising
  flour
2 teaspoons dry
  mustard powder
½ teaspoon chilli
  powder
125 g butter, chopped
½ cup grated Parmesan
  cheese
¼ cup water
milk for glazing
1 tablespoon sesame
  seeds

1 Preheat oven to moderate 180°C. Brush oven trays with melted butter or oil. Sift plain and self-raising flours, mustard and chilli into a large mixing bowl, add chopped butter. Using fingertips, rub butter into flour for 2 minutes or until mixture is a fine, crumbly texture, stir in cheese. Add almost all the water, mix to a soft dough, adding more water if necessary.
2 Turn onto lightly floured surface, knead for 1 minute or until smooth, shape dough into a log, 5 cm in diameter. Store, covered with plastic wrap, in refrigerator, 15 minutes. Using a sharp knife, cut log into 3 mm-thick rounds. Place on prepared trays, allowing room for spreading.
3 Brush rounds with milk, sprinkle with sesame seeds. Bake for 15 minutes or until lightly golden, loosen, cool on trays 5 minutes, transfer to wire rack to cool completely.

Note: Store biscuits in an airtight container for up to 1 week.
◆ Can be frozen for up to 2 months.

Chocolate Super Cookies (top), Chilli Cheese Biscuits

> ### HINT
> Chilli Cheese Biscuits are delicious served with cheese and pâté. This combination of goodies would make a great gift from the kitchen.

Lemon and Almond Shortbread Wedges

Preparation time:
15 minutes
Cooking time:
40 minutes
Makes 12 wedges

250 g butter
⅓ cup caster sugar
2 teaspoons grated
   lemon rind
1¾ cups plain flour
1¾ cups rice flour
½ cup ground almonds
sugar for sprinkling

1 Preheat oven to moderately slow 160°C. Brush an oven tray with melted butter or oil. Using electric beaters, beat butter, sugar and lemon rind until light and creamy.
2 Add sifted plain and rice flour and almonds, press together to form a soft dough. Turn onto a lightly floured surface, knead 5 minutes.
3 Roll dough into a 23 cm round using a cake tin as a guide, place onto greased tray.
4 Pinch a frill around the edge of the round. Use a large knife to score into 12 wedges. Prick evenly with a fork, sprinkle with sugar. Bake for 40 minutes or until lightly golden. Cut again, cool on tray.

Note: Store in an airtight container for up to 1 month.
◆ Shortbread can be frozen for up to 3 months.

Beetroot and Ginger Relish

Preparation time:
15 minutes
Cooking time:
1 hour 10 minutes
Makes about 4 cups

6 medium beetroot
   (1 kg)
1 cup sugar
2 cups white wine
   vinegar
1 onion, chopped
1 green capsicum,
   chopped
2 green apples, peeled,
   chopped
2 teaspoons grated fresh
   ginger
1 tablespoon seeded
   mustard

1 Place whole, unpeeled beetroot in a large pan, cover with water, bring to boil, cover, reduce heat to low, cook 45 minutes or until beetroot is tender, drain. Peel beetroot, cut into 1 cm cubes.
2 Combine sugar, vinegar, onion, capsicum, apple, ginger and mustard in large pan, bring to boil, reduce heat to low, cook uncovered for 15 minutes or until reduced by half.
3 Add beetroot, cook 10 minutes. Spoon into hot, sterilised jars, seal while hot.

Note: Store relish in refrigerator for up to 1 month.
◆ Unsuitable to freeze.

Curry Paste

Preparation time:
10 minutes
Cooking time: *6 minutes*
Makes 1 cup

2 tablespoons oil
1 onion, finely chopped
2 cloves garlic, crushed
2 teaspoons grated
   ginger
2 tablespoons ground
   coriander
1 tablespoon ground
   cumin
1 tablespoon dry
   mustard powder
1 tablespoon ground
   turmeric
1 tablespoon ground
   cinnamon
2 teaspoons chilli sauce
⅓ cup oil, extra
2 tablespoons vinegar
2 tablespoons lemon
   juice

1 Heat oil in a small pan, add onion, garlic and ginger, stir over low

Clockwise from left: Beetroot and Ginger Relish, Curry Paste, Lemon and Almond Shortbread Wedges.

heat until onion is soft.
2 Add coriander, cumin, mustard, turmeric and cinnamon, stir over low heat 2 minutes. Add chilli sauce, extra oil, vinegar and lemon juice, stir over medium heat for 3 minutes or until mixture thickens. Cool. Spoon into a sterilised jar, seal.

Note: Include a simple curry recipe (see right) with your gift.

Quick Chicken Curry

Serves 4
1 tablespoon oil
1 onion, *cut into eighths*
6 *chicken thigh fillets, cut into strips*
½ cup curry paste
½ cup coconut milk
2 tablespoons chopped *fresh coriander.*

1 Heat oil in a frying pan, add onion, stir-fry over high heat for 2 minutes.
2 Add chicken, stir-fry over high heat until browned. Add curry paste, stir-fry over high heat for 1 minute.
3 Add coconut milk, simmer uncovered for 10 minutes or until chicken is cooked and sauce thickened. Stir in coriander.

Caramel Nut Tarts

Preparation time:
 25 minutes
Cooking time:
 15 minutes
Makes 24

1½ cups plain flour
2 tablespoons cornflour
125 g butter, chopped
2 tablespoons water
⅔ cup sugar
2 tablespoons water, extra
⅓ cup cream
1½ cups roasted, unsalted mixed nuts, roughly chopped

1 Preheat oven to moderately hot 210°C. Brush shallow patty tins with melted butter or oil. Sift flour and cornflour into large mixing bowl, add chopped butter. Using fingertips, rub butter into flour for 2 minutes or until mixture is a fine crumbly texture. Add water, mix until combined. Turn onto a lightly floured surface, knead 1 minute or until smooth. Store, covered with plastic wrap, in refrigerator 10 minutes.
2 Roll pastry out thinly. Cut into circles using a fluted 7 cm round cutter, press circles into prepared tins. Prick pastry evenly with a fork. Bake 10 minutes or until lightly golden, cool.
3 Combine sugar and extra water in a small pan. Stir constantly over low heat until mixture boils and sugar has dissolved. Reduce heat, simmer, uncovered, without stirring 3 minutes or until golden. Remove from heat, add cream and nuts, stir until combined. Spoon into pastry cases, cool.

Note: Pastry cases can be made up to 3 days ahead. Filling can be added a day ahead. Store in airtight container.
◆ Unsuitable to freeze.

Date and Pecan Pinwheels

Preparation time:
 30 minutes
Cooking time:
 10 minutes
Makes about 35

1 cup chopped pitted dates
2 tablespoons sugar
¼ cup water
2 tablespoons chopped pecan nuts
90 g butter
½ cup brown sugar
1 egg yolk
1½ cups plain flour
½ teaspoon ground mixed spice
¼ teaspoon bicarbonate of soda
1 tablespoon milk

1 Preheat oven to moderate 180°C. Brush oven trays with melted butter or oil. Combine dates, sugar and water in a medium pan, stir over medium heat for 2 minutes or until water is absorbed. Remove dates from heat, stir in nuts, cool.
2 Using electric beaters, beat butter and brown sugar in small mixing bowl until light and creamy. Add egg yolk, beat until combined.
3 Add sifted flour, spice, soda and milk. Press together to form a soft dough. Turn onto lightly floured surface, knead 2 minutes until smooth. Leave, covered with plastic wrap, in refrigerator 30 minutes.
4 Roll out onto lightly floured surface to a rectangle 20 x 28 cm. Spread evenly with date mixture. Roll up from the long side. Wrap in plastic wrap, refrigerate 15 minutes.
5 Using a sharp knife cut log into 8 mm-thick rounds. Place on prepared trays,

Clockwise from left: Caramel Nut Tarts, Date and Pecan Pinwheels, Christmas Bells (p. 50)

allowing room for spreading. Bake for 10 minutes or until lightly browned. Cool on trays.

Note: Store in airtight container for one week.
◆ Pinwheels can be frozen for up to 2 months.
◆ You can vary the fruit and nut mixture. Raisins, mixed peel, prunes or sultanas can replace the dates, and walnuts, almonds or hazelnuts can be substituted for pecans.

Christmas Bells

Preparation time:
  30 minutes
Cooking time:
  10 minutes
Makes about 50

125 g butter
¾ cup caster sugar
1 egg
1¾ cups plain flour
1 teaspoon ground cinnamon
¼ cup cocoa powder
sugar for sprinkling

To attach bells to tree
10 m x 3 mm ribbon

1 Preheat oven to moderately hot 210°C. Brush oven trays with melted butter or oil. Using electric beaters, beat butter and caster sugar in small mixing bowl until light and creamy. Add egg, beat until combined.
2 Divide mixture between 2 small bowls. Add 1 cup sifted flour and cinnamon to one half, mix to a soft

1. *Christmas Bells. Beat butter and sugar, add egg, beat until combined.*

2. *Add remaining sifted flour and cocoa to half egg, butter and sugar mixture.*

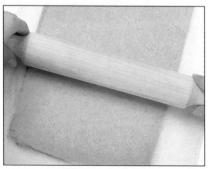

3. *Use a rolling pin to press the two mixtures together.*

4. *Cut mixture into bell shapes, cut a hole in top of each bell.*

dough. Add remaining sifted flour and cocoa to remaining half, mix to a soft dough. Store, covered with plastic wrap, in refrigerator 10 minutes.

3 Roll each mixture between 2 sheets of greaseproof paper to form rectangles, each measuring 20 x 30 cm. Remove top sheets of paper from each, invert one onto the other. Use rolling pin to press the 2 mixtures together, remove paper.

4 Cut into bell shapes using a biscuit cutter. Place onto prepared trays, allowing room for spreading, half with chocolate side facing up, remaining half with cinnamon side facing up.

5 Pile scraps on top of one another, roll out, cut into shapes, place onto prepared trays. Use a straw or small sharp pointed knife to cut a hole in the top of each bell. Sprinkle bells with sugar. Bake for 10 minutes or until lightly golden, loosen bells, cool on trays.

6 Cut ribbon into 20 cm lengths, thread through hole in top of bells, tie ends together in a knot.

Note: Bells can be made up to 3 days ahead, store in an airtight container.
◆ Bells made from the second rolling have a mottled appearance.
◆ Any shaped cutters can be used, e.g. stars, Santas, triangles and animals.
◆ Can be frozen for up to 2 months.

HINT
Use Christmas Bells to decorate your Christmas tree and let the kids have fun eating them during the festive season.

Florentine Slice

Preparation time:
15 minutes
Cooking time:
25 minutes
Makes 28

*2 cups cornflakes,
  lightly crushed*
1/2 cup sultanas
1/2 cup flaked almonds
*1/2 cup chopped glacé
  cherries*
1/4 cup mixed peel
2/3 cup condensed milk
*125 g dark chocolate,
  melted*

1 Preheat oven to moderate 180°C. Brush a deep 29 x 19 x 3 cm Swiss roll tin with melted butter or oil. Line base and sides with paper, grease paper.

2 Combine cornflakes, sultanas, almonds, cherries and peel. Add condensed milk, stir until combined.

5. Sprinkle bells with sugar. Bake for 10 minutes.

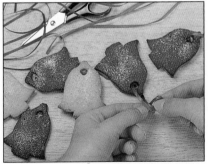

6. Thread ribbon through each hole, tie ends in knot.

3 Press mixture evenly into prepared tin. Bake for 25 minutes or until lightly browned, cool 5 minutes, turn out.

4 Cut into 4 x 4 cm squares. Hold each square by one corner, dip square halfway into chocolate. Allow excess to run off, place onto wire rack to set.

Note: Slice can be stored in an airtight container in refrigerator for up to 1 week.
◆ Unsuitable to freeze.

Mini Fruit Cake Pots

Preparation time:
15 minutes
Cooking time: *1 hour*
Makes six 2-cup pots

6 cups mixed fruit
1 cup glacé cherries,
  halved
250 g butter
1 cup brown sugar
1 cup water
5 eggs, lightly beaten
1 tablespoon grated
  orange rind
1³/4 cups plain flour
¹/3 cup self-raising
  flour
1 teaspoon bicarbonate
  of soda

1 Preheat oven to slow 150°C. Brush 6 x 2-cup terracotta pots with melted butter or oil.

Line base with a circle of paper, grease paper.

2 Combine mixed fruit, cherries, butter, sugar and water in a large saucepan. Stir over high heat until mixture boils, reduce heat to a simmer, cook, covered, for 10 minutes, stirring occasionally, cool.

3 Add eggs and rind. Stir until combined. Add sifted plain and self-raising flours and soda. Using a metal spoon, stir until just combined.

4 Spoon mixture into prepared pots, smooth surface, cover pots with aluminium foil. Bake for 1 hour or until cakes feel firm and are golden brown. Allow to cool in pots.

Note: Half the water can be replaced with rum, brandy or sherry.
◆ This mixture is enough to fill 4 nut roll tins.
◆ These cakes can be wrapped and stored in an airtight container for up to 1 month.

> ### HINT
> Include the pot in your gift. Remove the cake, wrap it in cellophane and put it back in the pot.

Grand Marnier Semolina Fruit Cake

Preparation time:
*20 minutes plus
  overnight soaking*
Cooking time: *4 hours*
*Makes one 23 cm
  round or one 20 cm
  square cake*

1¹/2 cups raisins, finely
  chopped
1¹/2 cups sultanas,
  finely chopped
1 cup mixed peel, finely
  chopped
1 cup finely chopped
  glacé apricots
¹/2 cup currants
¹/2 cup glacé ginger,
  finely chopped
¹/2 cup Grand Marnier
1¹/2 cups semolina
1 teaspoon ground
  cinnamon
1 teaspoon ground
  cardamom
185 g butter
4 eggs
1 cup brown sugar
¹/2 cup marmalade
¹/4 cup honey
3 teaspoons grated
  orange rind
¹/3 cup orange juice
1 cup slivered
  almonds

1 Preheat oven to slow 150°C. Brush a deep,

Clockwise from top left: Mini Fruit Cake Pots, Grand Marnier Semolina Fruit Cake, Florentine Slice (p.51)

23 cm round or a deep, 20 cm square cake tin with melted butter or oil. Line base and sides with a double thickness of paper.

2 Combine raisins, sultanas, peel, apricots, currants, ginger and Grand Marnier in a bowl, cover with plastic wrap, stand overnight.

3 Stir semolina in a saucepan, over medium heat for 5 minutes or until lightly browned. Add cinnamon, cardamom and butter, stir over heat until butter has melted, cool, cover with plastic wrap, stand overnight.

4 Using electric beaters, beat eggs and sugar in small mixing bowl until pale and foamy. Add marmalade, honey, orange rind and juice, beat until combined.

5 Transfer mixture to large mixing bowl, add fruits, semolina mixture and almonds. Using a metal spoon, stir until just combined.

6 Spoon mixture into prepared tin, smooth surface. Bake for 1 hour. Cover cake with a sheet of aluminium foil, reduce heat to very slow 120°C. Bake further 3 hours or until cake feels firm and is golden brown, cool in tin completely. Turn out, wrap cake so it is airtight and store.

Note: Dried fruits can be chopped in a food processor. Process each fruit individually. Be careful not to over-process or fruit will become mushy.

Traditional Fruit Cake

Preparation time:
*20 minutes plus
4 hours soaking*
Cooking time: *3 hours*
*Makes one 23 cm
round or one 20 cm
square cake*

*6 cups dried mixed fruit
1½ cups chopped dried
dates
1 cup chopped dried
apricots
1 cup chopped glacé
pineapple
¾ cup brandy
250 g butter
1 cup brown sugar
5 eggs
1½ cups plain flour
⅓ cup self-raising flour
1 teaspoon ground
cinnamon
blanched almonds for
decoration
glacé cherries for
decoration*

1 Preheat oven to slow 150°C. Brush a deep 23 cm round or a deep 20 cm square cake tin with melted butter or

oil. Line base and sides with a double thickness of paper.

2 Combine mixed fruit, dates, apricots, pineapple and brandy, cover with plastic wrap, stand at least 4 hours.

3 Using electric beaters, beat butter and sugar in small mixing bowl until light and creamy. Add eggs gradually, beating thoroughly after each addition.

4 Transfer mixture to large mixing bowl, add fruits, stir until combined. Using a metal spoon, fold in sifted flour, self-raising flour and cinnamon. Stir until just combined.

5 Spoon mixture into prepared tin, smooth surface. Decorate with almonds and cherries. Bake for 3 hours or until cake feels firm and is golden brown, cool slightly, turn out and cool completely. Wrap airtight and store.

Note: This cake can be wrapped and stored in an airtight container for up to 3 months.

HINT
For extra flavour, drizzle ¼ cup brandy over cake after removing it from oven.

Traditional Fruit Cake

Christmas Crafts

Christmas Tree Decorations

These hand-made felt Christmas decorations are great fun to make (the children can help), and are original and long-lasting. They could end up becoming Christmas heirlooms.

All decorations
coloured felt
embroidery thread in black and colours to match the felt
sequins and lace flowers
polyester fibre filling
gold thread or ribbon for hanging

1 Follow instructions on page 60 to enlarge patterns. Make patterns for all decorative felt shapes and allow a 3 mm seam on edges that are to be inserted on main shapes – mane and tail of the horse, comb of the hen and base of the tree.

2 Cut pieces from felt as described for each. Tack inserted pieces to wrong side of one main piece. Join main pieces using hand buttonhole-stitch in embroidery thread or with narrow machine zig-zag. Fill lightly before closing completely.

3 Stitch or glue decorations in place. Work embroidery, then thread tie with a large needle.

Chicken
Cut two of body and one each of comb and decorative pieces. Cut decorative pieces for other side if desired.

Cat
Cut two of body and one each of stripe and flower. Tie gold thread in a bow around neck.

Tree
Cut two each of tree and base, and one heart. Stitch a base to each tree piece, then make up as main piece.

House
Cut two each of house, window and sill, and one each of door and roof. Add roof and decorations after joining and filling main pieces.

1 sq = 1 cm

Horse

Cut two each of body and heart, one saddle on fold, one mane and a 5 x 1.5 cm tail. Cut end of tail in strips. Embroider eye on each side of head. Decorate saddle with a flower and heart.

Hearts and Flowers Tree

Gold pine cones and basket

Use gold spray paint and follow manufacturer's instructions to spray pine cones. Wear rubber gloves, as it is hard to avoid touching the cones while painting. When dry, wire cones to the tree. Spray a large cane basket gold as a container for the bucket holding your tree.

Gold garlands

These are gold curling ribbons loosely draped over the tree.

Angel

sheet of gold cardboard
pack of gold doilies
  with lacy edge pattern
6 cm white
  polystyrene ball
27 cm-long, 4 cm-wide
  cardboard cylinder
  (from plastic wrap)
gold curling ribbon
stapler
double-sided adhesive
  tape

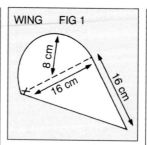

WING   FIG 1

8 cm

16 cm

16 cm

compass
ruler

1 Following Fig 1, make pattern for the wing, using compass and ruler.
2 On gold cardboard, draw a 30 cm-radius semi-circle and a concentric 3 cm-radius semi-circle; cut out this piece for body. Cut out two wings, a 50 x 5 cm strip for arms and a 6 x 3 cm piece to join the wings.
3 Overlap straight edges of body and join with double-sided adhesive tape. Insert cardboard cylinder through small neck opening, clipping neck edge for exact fit. Staple the edges together.
4 Stick centre of arm strip to back seam, about 7 cm from neck. Curve the arms to front and attach the ends to the angel's body on each side.
5 Cut one doily in half and arrange around

neck, stapling at back. Cut the decorative edge from a doily and drape over arms, sticking at back. Retain one doily for halo and cut the lacy edge from the rest to staple to edges of wings and lower edge of body. Attach wings to joining piece at X, then stick them to the back seam just above the arms.
6 Draw features on ball with felt-tipped pens or coloured pencils. Attach eight 40 cm lengths of curling ribbon to top of head with staple. Stick head to neck then stick the doily behind the head to form a halo.
7 To fix to tree, either push cylinder over tip of tree or, for extra support, tape cylinder to a length of dowel which you can wire to the tree.

Paper poinsettias
For about 28 flowers:
1 pack crepe paper
1 sheet red cellophane
1 roll 7-strand picture
  wire or fine
  gold-coloured wire
about 200 1 m
  sequins
fine wire-cutting pliers
stapler

1 Following instructions overleaf for

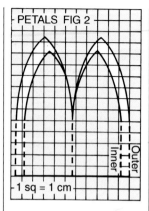

PETALS FIG 2

Inner
Outer

1 sq = 1 cm

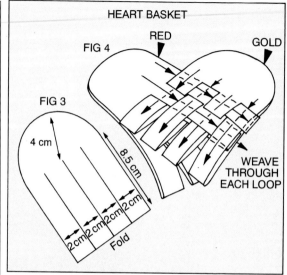

HEART BASKET

FIG 4
RED
GOLD

FIG 3

4 cm

8.5 cm

2cm 2cm 2cm 2cm

Fold

WEAVE
THROUGH
EACH LOOP

enlarging patterns, enlarge patterns for the petals, fig 2.

2 Fold crepe paper to the same width as large petal pattern and cut continuous strips of large petals. Do the same with cellophane and small paper pattern. Cut the petals into groups of six.

3 To make stamens, cut wire into 10 cm lengths, unwind one end of each piece of wire and attach a sequin to each strand, twisting twice with pliers to hold sequin. Or make up separate stamens from the fine wire and twist them together in groups of seven or more. Unravel some 10 cm lengths of wire to tie the flower petals in place.

4 To assemble flower, moisten straight edge of cellophane petals with a damp tissue to make them more pliable,

bunch around stamen wire and staple to hold. Gather crepe petals at base, arrange around cellophane, tie with wire. Holding sides of crepe petals, stretch each petal and push out its centre. Use the end of stamen wire to fasten the flowers to the tree.

Heart Baskets
For about 14 hearts:
1 sheet each red and gold firm, shiny gift-wrapping paper

cardboard
adhesive tape or stapler
scissors
metal straightedge
craft knife
compass
ruler

1 Using ruler and compass, draw pattern, fig. 3 on cardboard and cut out, using craft knife and straightedge for straight lines.

2 With pattern on fold of paper, cut, for each heart, one red and

How to Enlarge Patterns

On a sheet of paper, draw crisscross lines, vertically and horizontally, using a ruler and spacing lines as indicated. Copy one square at a time, using a ruler for straight lines. For curved lines, mark where lines intersect grid, and join.

one gold piece and a 2x16 cm strip for handle. While pieces are folded, make the 3 cuts with craft knife and straightedge. You can use scissors, but the craft knife is much quicker and neater.

3 Following Fig 4, weave strips together to form basket. Staple or stick end of handle securely to each side of the basket on the inside.

4 Tie heart baskets to tree with yarn or wire.

Christmas Topiary Tree

This little tree is made from ribbon bows. You could also use fabric cut with pinking shears and tied into bows, or tulle bunches.

ribbon bows in red,
*   white and green*
tree branch or dowelling
plastic plant pot
polystyrene ball
*   (available from florist*
*   or craft shops)*
firm florist's wire
*   (available from florist*
*   or craft shops)*
plaster of Paris
*   (available from*
*   hardware stores)*

1 Select a small tree branch for the trunk (or use a length of dowelling), sharpen one end and push the oasis ball firmly onto it.

Cover the holes in the bottom of the pot with plastic. Following directions on the bag, mix the plaster. Spoon plaster into pot and stand the tree trunk in the plaster. Hold steady until set.

2 Wind florist's wire firmly around centre of each bow, and push end into the oasis ball. It is important to get a good shape for the tree, so start by placing a top, bottom and two side bows to get the width of the tree. Turn tree around as you shape it, pushing bows in a little further or pulling them out a little to create the perfect shape.

3 Wire another large bow, push into base of

61

ball and allow ribbon to fall down the trunk.
4 Place tree in a painted basket and arrange coloured fabric around the base to hide the cement in the pot.

Shave Kit
Size: about 15 x 18 x 3 cm

33 x 53 cm piece of blue stripe fabric
18 x 56 cm piece of blue print fabric
46 cm of 115 cm-wide waterproof lining fabric (or nylon shower curtain fabric)
iron-on interfacing
30 cm zipper
15 x 30 cm stiff cardboard
1.5 cm seams allowed

1 From print fabric, cut two 18 cm square end pieces and one 8 x 18 cm strip. From lining, cut one 33 x 53.5 cm body, two 18 cm square ends, one 34 cm square. From interfacing, cut one 33 x 53.5 cm body and two 18 cm square ends.
2 Fuse interfacing to stripe body and end pieces. Baste lining to print end pieces. Baste a 5 cm box pleat at centre top of each end piece.
3 Fold 8 x 18 cm strip of print fabric lengthways right sides together. Seam, turn and cut in half. Fold in

half for tabs. Baste one, centred, over each pleat, matching raw edges.
4 With right sides together, centre and stitch zipper (5 mm seam) to 33 cm edges of body. Stitch print end pieces to body, right sides together, with zipper centred over tabs and clipping and pivoting at the corners.
5 With right sides together and edges even, pin lining to wrong side of zipper tapes. Stitch over previous stitching up to 1.5 cm from end pieces. Turn, machine-stitch lining closed to each of end pieces, clipping at corners.
6 Fold 34 cm square in half and stitch any two edges, turn right side out and turn in raw edges. Insert cardboard and stitch opening. Put into bag as a base.

Tote Bag
Size: 38 x 30 cm self-lined

1.5 m teal blue sailcloth or furnishing fabric
50 cm red sprig cotton
red and yellow remnants
25 cm heavyweight interfacing
1 cm seams allowed

1 Draw a heart on tracing paper, 10.5 cm down its centre length. Transfer to cardboard; cut out. Trace heart onto red remnant and cut 6 mm outside line. Tack heart shape, right side up, over cardboard. Press, remove tacking and cardboard.
2 Cut 23 cm square yellow pocket, hem 2 cm top edge. Centre heart on pocket, slipstitch.

3 From teal blue fabric, cut 40 x 148 cm bag bodies, two 15 x 62 cm sides. With right sides together, seam 40 cm ends together for centre bottom. Make marks 6.5 cm and 66.5 cm from both sides of seam, clip 1 cm at marks.

4 Match corners of one side piece to marks on body side, right sides together. Pin and sew all around. Repeat at other side, leaving 20 cm open. Turn bag through opening, slipstitch closed. Push half of bag inside other half to form self-lining (sides are 30 cm high). Press fold at top edge. Baste pocket to centre top on one side.

5 Cut 10 cm-wide sprig strips, seam to make 2.6 m ring for handle. Cut and seam interfacing the same way. Fold sprig strip around interfacing, turning raw edge under, slipstitch. Make another 23 cm sprig strip the same way, slipstitch to pocket bottom (see photograph), overlapping 1.5 cm. Mark halves of handle ring. Position on bag so marks are on centre bottom seam, 19 cm apart (handles overlap pocket sides 1.5 cm). Slipstitch in place.

Index